I Will Bear This Scar

I Will Bear This Scar

Poems of Childless Women

Edited by
Marietta W. Bratton

iUniverse, Inc.
New York Lincoln Shanghai

I Will Bear This Scar
Poems of Childless Women

iUniverse books may be ordered through booksellers or by contacting:

iUniverse
2021 Pine Lake Road, Suite 100
Lincoln, NE 68512
www.iuniverse.com
1-800-Authors (1-800-288-4677)

author photo credit: Stan Bratton

ISBN-13: 978-0-595-37124-2 (pbk)
ISBN-13: 978-0-595-81523-4 (ebk)
ISBN-10: 0-595-37124-8 (pbk)
ISBN-10: 0-595-81523-5 (ebk)

Printed in the United States of America

For my husband Stan
with special love for
Brooke and Shellee

Contents

Acknowledgments

There have been many people who sustained me on my healing road toward this book.

My husband Stan who always believed in me and pointed out the healing places to enjoy and share on the road. My sister Regina Abiles who has always listened and responded with honesty, creativity, and love. And of course, laughter. Wendy Baum for a friendship that celebrates our human heart. Lois Wolf for the richness in sharing thirty years of friendship, walking every step together.

I am deeply grateful to each of the women who submitted poems. Whether your work was selected or not, your words touched my heart.

PREFACE

"I just have to know. You're a teacher; your husband is a minister. Why don't you have children?" asked the allergist on my first and last visit to her office.

"You don't have children? Oh, I suppose your dogs are enough," remarked a co-worker.

Dealing with my childlessness has been a ten-year search for healing and connections with other women. Journaling, writing poetry, and reading have been my best resources. I've read more than twenty nonfiction books about childlessness, and these books have influenced my life in a positive way.

However, I remember my first response when I found a poem by a childless woman. I gasped and trembled, holding the paper in my hands as if it were sacred text. I could not take my eyes off the words until I had memorized at least two verses. I bought handmade paper and copied this poem by hand. Reading poetry about this experience was powerful for me. This was the beginning of my healing road toward this book.

At first I searched for poems by childless women whose voice would connect to my experience. I planned to copy their work by hand into a journal as a book for myself. As I worked on this, I realized that this journal was the book I had been searching for in every bookstore.

I Will Bear This Scar is the result of three years of encouragement from family and friends to write a book about childlessness. After a great deal of research and thought, I felt confident that other women would choose to give voice to their experiences in a collection of poems. I decided to offer these collective voices through an anthology.

I placed a call in *Poets & Writers Magazine* for poetry from women who had never had children. The response was immediate. In six months this call generated more than 200 submissions from poets across the United States, Canada, and England. Their poems and letters were moving and clear. Their work reflected the varied reasons for women to be childless: by choice, by delaying the decision until too late, not finding the right partner, abortion, miscarriage, and infertility. Their letters affirmed my belief. Childless women have a unique voice and deserve to be heard.

"...I jumped for joy that someone out there may be interested in my feelings about being childless."

"I'm glad to hear of it; it's a difficult subject, one that has not often been literarily explored."

"I was intrigued and heartened to see your call for manuscripts..."

"I think there are a lot of us out there dealing with the mixed feelings of being childless. Certainly there will be many more women in the future who could use some guideposts on this journey."

I invite you to read, listen to our voices, respond with yours, and know that you are connected to us.

After the Prelude

by Donna Frisk

Something happens to her
between ages 16 and 26. The tomboy
who wants nothing more
than to raise a bunch
of boisterous boys on a ranch
that spreads to all horizons
becomes cautious as an armadillo.

Perhaps she's too enamored
of her business suits and briefcase.
Perhaps she's learned that men
are wild geese who migrate
to more desirable climes.

Soon it becomes her composition,
as though she has written
the score. She never questions
whether the theme is her theme.
Till one day someone comes along
who wants a son.
In the passing of several moons
she and the life inside
are unsettled by the discordance.
He chooses to not be born.

She picks up her baton,
continues from where she left off.
The symphony of her life
moves between the happy frenzy

of gypsy music and lullaby and lament,
ending on notes every bit
as satisfying as a baby's first cry.
The audience applauds.

Andromeda at Mid-Life

by Ann Cefola

Why do I read my daily horoscope,
the sun's angle cast over lines, planets telling me
to avoid purchases or commitments?
I want to believe in this cosmic dance,
that slow-radiating waves pull at me like tides,
arrange a telephone call from someone I haven't heard from
in six years. Looking at the constellations, or the ring around Saturn,
I need to believe in a pattern, a higher order, a face with designs
upon me, like the alarm that wakes me each day, reporter breathless
with 6:30 a.m. crises. The idea that light so far away could ever reach or
influence me. I could study tea leaves but I like the bigness up there,
the regularity of Orion arriving each winter, the exhaustion of Perseus running.
I think there is room for me too, a constellation, a myth, a woman of 43
constantly looking up and wondering, who realizes at last
the dipper is full, the hunter will never catch the bear and
Andromeda must unloose her own chains, rub her rusty wrists,
stretch, then sit down and cast her future in stars.

Angela

by Robens Napolitan

To lose a little girl,
not quite made,
her body flushed from mine
before her birth time,
is the only nightmare I can remember.

Now, many years later, I wonder
who this daughter might have been.
Is her spirit still waiting to be born,
or have I seen her face in passing, stopped
to admire her beautiful eyes and curls?

I wonder anew at the pain of loss which,
even now, can wrench me out of sleep.
I never held her, or heard her call me "Mommy,"
but I was a mother once, until the blood
ran down my legs and she was gone.

Apples and Oranges

by Lauri Rose

This is your life:
Disposable income,
Two cats
And the comfort of a good book
You can read without hiding in the bathroom.

The mortgage is paid off.
And you never had to wait up at night
Wondering if your child was still a virgin.

On the other hand
No one ever ran to you
Because only you
Could make it better.

Instead you went to every one of Sara's chemo sessions
While others attended soccer games
And school plays.

Of course,
They would have comforted you in your old age.
(Though Barbara's only asks for money).
Certainly they would have laughed
At your first pair of glasses.

On the couch,
With a glass of wine
You decide with annoyance
(Or is it regret?)
That this is a little like
Comparing apples and oranges
An ultimately futile activity.

Baby:

by Karla Linn Merrifield

It could have been any grocery store,
any produce aisle, any onion

held in her hand to her nose
when the rush of fluid & human

embryo gushed down her thighs
to the floor: Her young husband thought

the uncut Vidalia had caused her
to cry. In the midst of greens—lettuces,

spinach, watercress, basil & chives—she
watered the scene with emerald tears

for the green inchoate thing at her feet
Now all those vegetables have been eaten,

or rotted, or supplanted by heartier hybrids
these sixteen harvest seasons since.

But you know how old it'd be today,
don't you, *my petite choufleur?*

Balancing on a Shaft of Sunshine

by Marianne Poloskey

This is one of those pictures
we retrieved from a relative
years later. There, dressed
in white, is my brother.
A tiny boy plump as a puppy,
he stands off by himself,
mouth open, hands raised
as if applauding. My mother,
though the most important person
in the picture, manages as usual
to remain in the background,
blending right in with her dark coat,
almost engulfed by the shadows of war.
I am close to her, leaning my head
against her side, balancing
on a shaft of sunshine
that runs like fire along the ground.
I remember that moment so well—
how cold it was, with the trees
barren and unable to hide us,
yet I felt safe in the park and wished
I wouldn't have to go indoors again.
And I remember the photographer,
a patient man stomping his feet,
blowing into his hands to keep warm,
breath escaping his mouth like smoke.
He kept pleading with me to look up
and smile into the camera
until there was a crack in his voice.
But I couldn't.
I was still shaky from the air raid
the night before, and from the promise

I made to myself—that if I survived,
I would never bring children
into this world.

The Barren Wife

by Erin Garstka

In Wales if the ivy failed, it meant that the house would
pass into other hands, probably through infertility.
   —Sheila Pickles, <u>The Language of Flowers</u>

Lone blue evening against the Pacific,
you were a woman at supper with twelve sailors,
your hunger transparent as a host of moon,
hope lost, a rusted anchor dropt in swollen surf.

Arid consort of marauding gypsies,
you trailed mirages to an oasis,
slept on burning sands until fiery visions
left your body a column of ashes, smoke.

Two husbands and no squalling babe to bear
a name beyond these walls, you are mother of none
but a shame that mimics ecstasy or grief,
troublesome as a tooth that must be pulled.

Plant ivy. Wield whips of tiny green hands,
weave them round a wooden stake, form crowns of stars—
leaves spiked, outstretched, white-edged as constancy,
singular as earth calling for your return.

Biting Lemons

by M. Tracey Chesler

I thought I felt…*that way*
in the shower, my puffy tummy
why am I so tired all the time?

while dressing in the doorway
you come behind me and I'm Marilyn Monroe
why am I eating all of this?

slipping my foot into a shoe
the blue polished tootsies, swollen teeny tiny cleavage tidbits
why don't I drink more water?

how long has it been,
one day
two
three maybe, no two
I thought I felt…*that way*

floating to the drug store
two days, time for the test
I'll take it on the toilet in the morning

the satin nightgown tonight
tomorrow could be Christmas morning
don't you think my face is filling out?

I can't sleep, give me the covers
I'm hugging you
because you're with me

I can do this………wait………a baby?
a minus sign………hmmmmmmmm, not this time
my hope turns sour, like when you bite into a lemon

"honey hand me the box of tampons please"
no pink booties…no receiving blankets…no christening gowns to
unpack
in a few days I'll slim back down

and ache for a different sign
the next time
I feel…*that way.*

Blessing of the Black Virgin

by Rachel Dacus

I am ready to park my useless womb
in a pew in the Church of Wellbeing. Swaying,
still drunk from lunch and pasta-queasy, I sit
with blanked vision in marble dark,
blinded by San Marco's televised Mother's Day Mass.
Snapped-out with shots of tots on Venice's stone lions,
depleted from cramps, I sink into a Black Madonna's gaze.

My husband's thigh presses on mine. Thoughts
leach together: jet lag and luck's pull-dates,
a void where the swelling should be.
The Madonna's eyes poke and prod,
grazing down from her gold foil heaven,
So you want to be a mother?
Her halo pricks tears from my pinched lids
and she holds out an emerald studded box
whose crowned lid does not exactly fit.

Arms rise up beyond the frame,
pulling us all down. Her words rumble
below the marble. *I bring them all
into being. Just climb down into my dark boat.*
The floor spins, mosaics arrowing out
and I toss our canceled children
into an unknown virgin's lap.

Outside in sun, we wait beside the bone-brightness
for a vaporetto. How did I arrive here?
I was brought up believing everything was mine
to make—even, certainly, children.
Restless as water, I catch a last murmur
from inside as The Lady of Last
Chances throws a boon: In heat shimmer
above the lagoon, her grant rises:

Be a mother, then—be singed and blackened
tending the flame of a child in every ear and eye.

Blood-Cycle Brooding

by Rachel Dacus

One more unpeeling of the womb,
close enough to the final time
that I can relish the tiny tearings,
the way muscles unclasp
from what might have been—
One more the shredding of a bed
that waited fruitless five times seven
years for an egg and dart
to decorate its aching lap.

Once more a blood-gravity pulls
me into a planet's centripetal spin,
the dropping-down cramp
mimicking birth-pang,
open mouth delivering
a new poem, breath
heaving and rasping.
And what do I have left
from all those empty moon-circles?

Scraped squeaky clean, the blood-room
has birthed generative words.
They sleep twitching in their cradles
or sun themselves nude on public rocks.
Tribe after diatribe of oaths and chants
spilled from lips too like another portal.
Yes, in this blood-tide of verbs
I brought myself forth
through a mirror, witched awake
out of the pounding dark.

Bloodknot (Spenserian Stanza)

by Sharon Griffiths

The flesh is nothing more than cloud. The cloud
congeals around a stone inside, a pear
upturned and floating—pulsing, singing loud
in blood-song wordless as the primal air
allowing it to glow, the outside there
illuminated hot, the furnace of
creation. Inside, night seems not to care,
its space spreads cold and curved, ignoring love
with points of light that swell and sparkle, burst above

Like fireworks in silver monochrome.
The sparks, the seeds exploding, never nest.
And once a month, there is a moon, full-grown
that pauses, passes out of sight, addressed
to no one, silent as a bone, unblessed.
Despair crowds in like famine—not this time,
another month is washed away in rust
and gusts of air. The womb commits the crime.
The heart, with neutral blood, is only marking time.

"But What Do You <u>Do</u>?"

by Peggy Lin Duthie

I grow Witness in my garden
and other flowers groomed without names.
I cultivate the purrs of my cat
and cup my palms around my inadequate ears.
I peer at my house's nests of wires and cables,
calm in their tangles, yet simmering with news
a-strut in rumor's fresh finery.
And then I study the slants of my blinds:
how they make the sunlight special,
how it warms my chosen silence.

"But What _Will_ You Do?"

by Peggy Lin Duthie

When I am an old woman,
I'll eat purple popsicles,
Strolling plump and naked
Across my apartment's
mild and gracious silence
of ancient books
and beautiful, breakable vases.

Channeling Bryce

by Rikki Santer

Once they branded her barren,
she craved for a ripple
melding into honor,
a space brimming
with fresh corpuscle,
promise of small fingers
welding hearts.

She put a name to her ambition:
Bryce, you will be alert and
swift, the street where my parents
began their love.

So she beckons you
from beyond the cold night stars
many blocked
by light of too much city.

HMO faxes her empty hands
cold shoulder.
Herbalist advises plantain
blessed thistle
translucent jewels of wheat germ
all the while prescribing a zen dismissal
of crouched purpose.

She channels through moments of her days
trying to conjure the stanza that will swell you.
Are you nestling
    behind the gaze of a lover?
Skating atop the mirror
    she glimpses sideways?
Saturating the breath of a page
    ready to be turned?

Chaos

by Lisa Beatman

The bedrock broke when baby died,
and the elements could not help but shift.
My husband turned to stone, I to water.
The sob sac burst at my feet this time,
and rose and raged through what was once hometown.
My husband sank, I envied his sure direction,
I could not staunch the umbilical slash
I surged and spewed, spurted and eddied,
sucked in the muddied sky, and time
ran out, vortexed in bedlam tides.
No breath could catch beneath the breaking waves,
no Noah chart an unshored course, no dove
or twig, no dim horizon, brim to hold me,
and all unformed
and vaporized
and there was
darkness
upon the face
of the
earth.

Child of War

by Marianne Poloskey

I am a child of war,
born in the zig-zag of lightning,
in the zig-zag of *Blitz*,
the *Blitzkrieg* that turned
in on itself
like a boomerang.

At night, while bombers razed cities,
poets sat in their rooms
erasing errors—
and our beds turned cold.

Those days of fairytales
with their unhappy endings

made me fragile but tough—
a wildflower living
in its own scars,
whose neck will not snap
as long as it has
enough tears to drink.

I will tell you my story, Doctor,
but please do not try
to make me forget,
do not take it away
like a hurt.
This is my childhood.
This is all I have.

Christmas Tree

by Susan Landon

Tangled in the branches
of a Vermont pine
are the terrors
of thirty years.

I bury my body
in layers of sweaters
woven by women
around the world.

I adorn my tree
with the barest
of ornaments:
a filament of hope.

I am alone,
and celebrate
my oneness.

Constant Comment

by Patricia McMillen

Fourteen years later, I know that you
were never angry, never blamed me—as
even, sometimes, I blamed myself—you
never judged. And yet, each morning, when
you'd lift your heavy head from the pillow,
place one foot, then the other, on the bare
wood floor, saying nothing—nothing at all—
pull blue jeans over knees, buckle your belt,
creak down the stairs to start tea—I heard
it all, each word you didn't say, until
the kettle sighed and you opened the hinged
lid of our wooden tea box, found it empty.
Then I felt—you'd nowhere else to put it—
the full weight of your disappointment.

Dark Night

by Patricia McMillen

O sharp-edged poem, square-headed,
unrepentant: in giving birth to you
I sustain further damage.

In bearing you, awkward, malformed
lines, my unhappy womb
stretches into ever more grotesque

shapes; the edges of my mouth
rip and bleed.
You emerge at the wrong time

and place: back seat of a taxicab,
deserted cornfield in the dead
of winter. Uncalled, uncalled-for

child disowned by your father,
you leave me bloody,
cracked and resewn. Yet you

are all the child I'll ever have;
grateful, I press your hard mouth
to my breast.

The Daughter I Don't Have (1)

by Lyn Lifshin

could be my other,
following me on the
subway, in the car.
She hovers like a
cloud over the lilacs,
a cloak over plum
branches. She moves
like a warm front
east, is that buzz
in the night, out
of reach in blackness.
I've known her sting,
how she tangles in
my hair, that, with
me, she will forget
I fought her, forget
her wandering and
waiting like bees
that lose all memory
of their old hive
once they've swarmed

The Daughter I Don't Have (2)

by Lyn Lifshin

will have strong
Georgia O'Keeffe
hands that could
carry what she
needed, would
know when to
let go. She'd
feel plum light
in a treeless
slope, could
listen for hours
to the night
sounds of the
prairie, not
need a world
with roads. The
daughter I
don't have would
smell sun on her
skin, could
walk away from
movie theaters,
galleries, feast
on the iridescence
of shooting stars,
shapes like blue
lace moving into
shadows and like
O'Keeffe, see only
the curves and
textures—
not death in
bleached skulls

Do You Know What It Is To Lose a Shadow?

by Barbara Hantman

Do you know what it is to lose a shadow?
Misplaced: one sweet and innocent appendage
That tinkers with the toolbox
And flutters from nursery to kitchen
In search of papa's praise and guidance.

Do you know what it is to lose a shadow?
Canceled: one proud-as-a-peacock bar-mitzvah boy strutting to the bimah,
One Isaac ben Avraham married under a flat-bed expanse of glimmering
                              desert stars,
The reassuring warp and weft of nomadic branches caught in a green-
                              bowered chupah,
The shattered wine glass sending forth fragments of tenderness and
                              passion
That make an elixir of delight for each of Rachel's daughters.

Do you know what it is to lose a shadow?
(The ache in the gut that never abates)
Alas, no! I never had a shadow.

Early for the Dance

by Amy Minato

Look. I know you
enter the room. You are
in one corner waiting, egg-
white dress against the red
carpet, folds in folds

of chromosomes, dreamy
as a sheep. Quit
rushing me. I told you.

Your partner's not here.
The music's not on yet.

Eve's Legacy

by Jenn Monroe

I.
lost my girlish figure at 29
happened overnight, i swear
my hips moved down and out
mother said
i lost my figure when—

i don't have a baby

II.
after three years
now on a list
built a nursery this year
soft yellow walls
with mint green rocking horses
furniture in unfinished pine

they keep the door open

III.
latex allergy
almost killed by birth control pills
deep vein thrombosis
twelve days before Christmas
doc says if i got pregnant
it would be high risk

IV.
a childless woman is
at greater risk for
breast cancer
incessant maternal badgering
inappropriate questioning

suicide
homicide

V.
she wanted a baby
a fertility specialist said
she was not mentally fit

she was in his lot when he came out
standing barefoot on sticky asphalt
pointed a gun at her head
he came closer
she lowered the gun
smiled and
shot

VI.
i think i babble when i wake up
strangers stare
their mouths gape in disgust
another female patient cries
as a man strokes her hair like a cat
did i tell?

suddenly, hands
whip close
the curtain between us

Fertility Rights

by Mindy Lewis

A work in clay—
female figure, full-breasted,
This sculpture flaunts what I try to conceal-
Irrepressible swelling of reproductive questions.
My tired brain, concentrated, full
Breasts lost among paperwork, deadlines-
I am like the bound woman of ancient East,
The hidden body only revealed each day
After unwrapping yards and years of paper bondage;
Womb only released later, when in the bath
I strive to look only at my naked toes,
Ignoring those other parts breaking the water's surface,
Each breast a pointed question awaiting a blunt answer.

First Trimester

by Katherine Cottle

The desert roses have not returned,
unlike the rest of the blooms,
broken under the wild grass and weeds
covering the front bed.

This year, a set of purple lips
opened instead,
growing inches overnight
between the tulip stems
and brittle forsythia.

Inside, everything moves
and is still.
The clock ticks,
the calendar gets crossed off,
breakfast becomes lunch
becomes dinner.
I take the wild bloom,
leave its long stem
smothered in the water
of a tall vase.

Within hours it has wilted,
the wetness dripping off its petals,
its soft pink center
too drenched and tired
to hold its weight any longer.

Flying Solo

by Lisa Beatman

I love to fly, to be between
The past obscured, future unseen

Strapped in waiting, cupped in motion
Flight attendants' deep devotion

Office flurry left behind
Itinerary undefined

The paper's stopped, the mail as well
My creditors can go to hell

Ensconced in *now*, no obligations
Just movies, magazines, c-rations

My seatmates I can take or leave
Unless it's necessary to relieve

Myself, it's just a question
Of quelling any indigestion

And unlike hometown complications
Row 9 members enjoy relations

Predicated on the plan
We'll never see each other again

Transient intimacies unfold,
Emboldened, on a stranger's shoulder

I must admit a secret pleasure
in knowing that I must endeavor

To endure others' bambinos
Only 'til we land in Reno

London, Lisbon, or L.A.
Then grab my bags and go my way

And thence to board another dream
Aloft, adrift, alone, serene.

Forty-five This Spring

by Alison Townsend

All this year I have secretly been growing old,
the ovaries spilling their last burgundy stain,

dark as wild blackberries I plunged my hands into
twenty summers ago, heedless of scratches.

They've been shutting down when I wasn't watching,
closing up shop while I plotted the possibility of a child

at mid-life, estrogen's lightning line disappearing
fast as dust in rain. No hot flashes or night sweats,

no blood-flood breaking the uterus-dam,
nothing but me and this sputtering body

that still fits, even betrayed by the moon.
Dark veils slide across her farthest silver reaches

like mirrors in a house where death sits down
and visits for a long time before leaving.

O moon! O Hecate, gate-keeper, cave-dweller,
one-who-knows-her-way-in-the-dark, goddess

of crossroads and young things, why must it end?
I fold up names of children inside me—

Elizabeth, Phoebe, Rebecca, Simone—
the way my sister and I once folded antique

baby clothes we found in a trunk in the barn,
as if they came from another life too precious

to be worn in ours. Their syllables follow me
like small ghosts; they cling to every thorn.

Fruit

by Amy Dengler

This morning I washed strawberries,
cleaving each red heart in half
until a hill of ruby chunks rose in the red bowl.
I carved Granny Smiths into quarter moons, sliced
black-seeded kiwis, snipped in green grapes luminous
as sea eggs.

We meet at noon.
The baby clings to my sister, Sarah, like a koala cub.
He blows fierce raspberries, then burrows into Sarah's shoulder,
his hair orange feathers against her green shirt.

Vicky's four are at school
but I see them in the open leaves of their library books,
their mitts and bats scattered like orchard windfall.
They'll be home at three, all legs and shouts
backpacks and baseball caps.

Sarah scoops chicken salad onto china plates,
Vicky slices Italian bread, unwraps a stick of butter.
I spoon out fruit and brew tea; amber splashes
in iced glasses.

We pull up chairs and pass the baby,
talk above the quiet clatter
of silver, the clink of ice.
The sun moves in yellow cubes across the table.

Later we load the dishwasher, pack up rattles,
orphaned socks, wooden blocks and baby bottles.

<u>Don't forget your red bowl</u>...

Vicky hands it to me.
It is so light
I might be carrying nothing.

Gazelle

by Shushan Avagyan

Gilded with apricot dust—they are moist seedpods
my ovaries : ready to be loved : caressed in the waters of *Van*[1]—

my ovaries—red—

like the color of genocide : a pomegranate ripped apart
ruby streams gushing

                              from my ovaries.

These lesions : scars : cuts : bruises :: never healed
(how could they) turned into baggage too

                              heavy to carry

I am sorry to tell you—the voice said in the check up room—
your ovaries—they are deformed—
they are not normal—(take these numbers

                              for surrogate mothers)
instead you could write.

Write down an umbilical word. Breastfeed each sentence.
Nurture the commas,

                    stroking the empty sheets of paper-skin
with velvety palms—
every time I push harder : a metonym emerges

and then I start bleeding again-

---

[1]   A native lake and a town in Ottoman Turkey where my paternal grand-
       mother was born, and from where she fled during the 1915 Armenian mas-
       sacres

Going North

by Lonnie Hull DuPont

i.

Leaves twist on the ground,
scraping,
louder than the wind. Over Lake Michigan
the flat red sun
sinks into Milwaukee.
By morning
I find the leaves
in a circle beneath my window.

ii.

I drive north to the straits
through pine and birch,
past white dunes and beaches
of petosky stones.

I find the 45th parallel
near a shop full of shells.
I ask the shopkeeper
about ghost towns I remember.

She claims they are inhabited now.

iii.

I have said
the lakes are like oceans,
but this is not true.
Lakes have no tides, they have
driftwood, bleached and hollow,
whitecaps bright as seagulls.
Lakes are clear, uncomplicated.

Open your eyes underwater
and see only sand.

iv.

Under a hanging light bulb
waving in the harbor wind,
my brother-in-law filets salmon,
calls me to him. *See*, he says,
this one was female. He points
with his knife. Rosy eggs,
a voluptuous spilling of them,
like so many pearls. Wet, shining. All lost.

v.

When ships go down in Superior
they are never found.
So deep, so cold, imagine
that littered floor, iron tankers
creaking like old trees, corpses
perfectly preserved, all eyes
open.

When ships go down in Superior
no whales sing to the dead.
But south in Onekama
swans keep a vigil through silent fog.

Gone: What I Dreamed After the Abortion

by Alison Townsend

I was holding my baby when I stood at the bottom
of the steep marble stairs before the great woman poet:

I was holding my baby when I looked up into the clear,
pitiless eyes of she whom I believed gave permission to write;

I was holding my baby as I ascended, the marble
veins freezing in each stair beneath me;

I was holding my baby as the poet opened her arms,
like great wings or a cape of light woven from darkness;

I was holding my baby as I went up, one slow step at a time
from the underworld that looks like the town where I live;

I was holding my baby—even on the last step—of this I am certain,
I was holding my baby, her weight sweet and easy in my arms;

I was holding my baby as the poet spread her wings;

I was holding my baby as I walked inside the circle
the feathered cape made around us; I was holding my baby,

then I was above ground, but my baby had vanished;
not a cry in the air, not even the memory of a cry,

and how often I've wished for a pebble or splinter of wood,
something to stop me before I reach that last step

and open my arms, to the great poet in silence;
nothing but a child-shadow slipping into the wet black

behind us, while the great poet anoints me,
placing her arms around me like the mother she is not.

The Good Wife

by Dianna Vagianos Miller

The good wife cleans brown stains
from the toilet seat, she washes
the yellowed underwear,
the silty solid milk in the blue
tumbler.

She goes to the farmer's market
and gathers sorrel, amaranth
and lavender, she nurtures
those around her table with broth
and berries.

The good wife gives away
her last chocolate chip cookie,
her last bar of cream white soap,
her last daylight hours to other people's
children.

She would have bought a butterfly
cookie for her daughter. Jane, crack
the cookie on your forehead. See
orange and purple sugar fall
to the floor.

The Grief of Solace

by Reeves Keyworth

In the dream, she is a child
of six or seven. It is joy
to pull her to me, place
her backside against my knees,
and lift her straight brown hair
away from the nape of her neck:
my gesture makes us two a refuge.
There is a garland given
to indicate this scene:
"I Cut the Hair
of My Thoughtful Daughter, Po."
For a moment, she is indeed thoughtful,
shy and patient, then
she shakes her head like a pony,
and though I take hold of her arm,
she's gone from my grasp.
I cannot keep her.

One arrow of interpretation
points to life's resolute
noli me tangere. Her name
might be a watchword
for poetry or the poet Li Po,
who drunken meanders
under the T'ang Moon
have always given me the shiver
of a far and beginningless time.
But under my hand,
her arm was warm and rounded,
and my desire to protect her
was not symbolic.
She fled with the quick
confident twisting of spirit
that loosens all obedience.

In my youth I had nightmares
—falling plunges, armed men—
but now, when readying age
holds the gun to my head,
dreaming, I conjure
a beautiful willful daughter
whose loss I still grieve for,
many waking days later.

Grief's Place

by Carol Tufts

Rejoice, O barren one who has not given birth.
For more numerous are the children of the forsaken
than the children of the favored wife.
   —Tractate Berakhot

Grief's Place says the sign
above one more outdoor stand
shuttered for the season
along the greying Maine coasts
we browse, intemperate
tourists, the wintering
Grief, miles south, tricked
out in some palm-splashed
shirt, all flash against the prim
pressed Florida sand.

Marooned here at Grief's closed place
we bend into the wind's rough bite,
the salt stench of gull-stripped fish
and sea debris, each of us
looking off to some separate point,
and I imagine you again
remembering her, your wife
before me, the way she kept you
doting and close
to home, her fears coiled
fine as a life's work.

She would not have dreamed
me here with you
at Grief's Place this fall
of our tenth year, my body
yielding to that barrenness
which is my curse
in loving you, this simple gift
you made of it to her,
unthinking, the two of you
with children enough.

Around us the wooded hills are dying
into their autumn ecstasy
where the day's late light embraces them
as we move toward each other,
gathered to a landscape
where everything is dancing,
the dazzled leaves spinning
like blowing embers, or the luminous
ashes of my fallow flesh,
lifting in the quickening wind
of another coming spring.

The Gypsy

by Jacqueline Sentmanat

She sat and waited
A cool Fall day on the Venice boardwalk
Basking in the glow of my new-found city,
I took her challenge to divine my future
And gave my hand as I sat at her table

Long life, she smiled
You will circle the globe countless times she pronounced
You will know wealth, in time, she said knowingly
Then, almost as an aside, she uttered
You will be surrounded by children, but none of them will be yours.

My future held promise
To fly to great places and see marvelous things
She may have said something of a fantastic love
But I could not focus
My head was spinning from her curse.

You will be surrounded by children, but none will be yours.

Barren, apparently, barren by choice
Was the cost of my fortune the dream of my child?
The child so real to me she suckled my breast while I slept
The baby quilt in the hope chest rotting while smelling of cedar
A dream shattered by a half-baked gypsy

None will be yours.

Look again I hissed
Pleading inside for some lame validation
She turned the hand around then looked at the other palm
Her still unpaid fee rested in my pocket
She quickly murmured about some child being of my own.

A decade has passed, I now wonder if perhaps she meant my dog

Travels have taken me far
I enjoyed the wealth of love and fortune
Scores of children call me "Auntie"
Included in families bonded by blood or wisely chosen
Recitals, school plays and holidays surrounded by children

None of them mine, except the furry one.

But that cool, Fall day I sighed in fragile comfort
And rose before she took back her vision
Paid her fee as she smiled gratefully
Walking down the boardwalk, feeling the wind on my face
And silently wished her dead.

I Will Bear This Scar

by Marietta W. Bratton

this scar
    sign of healing

this scar
    way of remembering

a closing of
    an opening to

The Judgment

by lu carter

The man who examined
my uterus in the laboratory
said it looked perfectly normal,
wondered why they'd torn out
my shiny scarlet room,
its walls never stretched by fetus
or bruised by kicking feet.

Why'd you let them take it,
he asked, as if I'd watched
as masked men snatched
screaming infants from strollers
in the city park.
I begged them to, I answered,
tried to describe the pain
that filled the silent place inside
like a big-breasted soprano singing
the opera's highest notes,
shaking the red plaster down,
never stopping for a breath.
I told him about the clots and painkillers,
the poking and prodding by perplexed doctors
with fingers too pudgy to fit me.

Well, it looked perfectly normal, he said,
and walked away.

The Kids Speak

by Barbara Daniels

These are the kids
I never had,
arrogant and smart.
Rebellious punks,
they jump on couches,
smoke in bed,
spill grape juice
on the rug, steal
from drug stores
and from me.

Here they are,
as many as there
might have been,
reciting their
mean litany
of blame. You
went out too much,
stayed in too much,
they say. You
never loved us
half enough.
You're fat.

You never even
had us, never
wanted to. You
closed your legs,
refused the sperm,
or jumped right up
to wash each chance
of us away.

Kore

by Dianna Vagianos Miller

I forgot about you, kore,
until I smeared a streak
of subtle blood on my towel.
I had conceived you already
savoring a glass of Chianti, under the eyes
of my poet cat, in my grandmother's bed
while the moon shifted and sighed.
I dreamt of releasing you, daughter
into the life I thought I had given you
all along.

Lilith in Spring

by Rhoda Janzen

Moss patches the oak with green
distraction, shivering beards where
crotch meets undressed limb,
forever considering contagions

in the clouds. Is your leaf carpet
shagged with frost? Your acorn
mound rubbled under snow panties,
the underblush one confesses

to the curb—winter's leavings,
broken silver sorrows that squall
like naked shoulders to no natural sun?
Do you want to be caught? Do

you want to fall, to freezefall and thaw,
forgotten, spilled seed crushing
Sanseoy and Samongelof on the cusp
of spring? The sky vows to be

your weather forever, it is yours,
it loves you, pet it, it wants to sniff
your ice. Crocuses spear the garden
with surprise. Strike the sleeping

stems like lips with one finger—
the debris of winter, born and half-born,
dying and dead, my lilim, the babies
I never wanted, the whirlwinds that I had.

Lines to My Son, If He Had Lived

by Ruth Moon Kempher

Become what you will, there's a mix
stringing behind you, of all the possible

beginnings, you could try anything
but someone before you will have

been at it, years back, more than likely.
Be patient with your elders, for that.

Be a planter—be a sower of ideas—
or of seeds, raising fields of white-flowered

peas—or golden alfalfa, for feed. Nourish
all creatures who come to you; plant

trees, especially the fruitful, cherries or
oranges or pears. Or work with your hands.

Be a craftsman, with wood or words.
Be a maker of new things. Or travel. Be free.

My mother was a traveler, always over seas.
She'd say: keep your passport in a safe pocket.

Drink only stuff from bottles. Wine or water.
Local bread is always good; also pasta.

Her father sailed from Lithuania, he a tailor
and maker of hats, a sewer of seams.

Become what you will.
Be cautious. Be brutal. Dream.

Meditation

by Mary Sue Koeppel

Wise men do not grieve
having discarded sorrow.
   —Dhammapada

Sorrow is to be discarded,
not thrown out like garbage,
not fingered or sorted
or given to the less fortunate,
but discarded like old cells,
like flakes of skin in the shower,
discarded like long hair
wound through a pointed comb.

A part that is not a part
anymore is not grieved.
Wise ones neither mourn,
nor weep, nor squint in pain,
but sit in sacred stillness.
Peace is the quiet discarding.

Memorial Lights

by Carol Tufts

My mother lights the *yarzheit* lamps,
the glasses of flickering candle wax
a toast offered the dead
to kindle this day of remembrance,
warming to life again
her parents,
a bachelor uncle,
a barren aunt
jangling inside her costume jewelry

How they crowd the table
these dead, the spent heat
of their lives filling the air
like their voices once
joined over an evening meal.

They will whisper to darkness,
each small lamp, each day to follow
as it strikes nearer to flame,
my mother coming to burn at last
among the rest. And childless
as that aunt we quicken now
by our remembrance, I will gather to me
all my dead to glow through the long hours,
lighting my way.

Moth Wings

by CB Follett

There were children once.
They came in the nights.
To some I assigned
all our best features;
to others
all the worst:
then loved them each.

I spun them toy boxes of balsa
and comforters of moth wings.
I stocked the larder with
Good and Plenties
and mugs of frothed milk.

All my shelves were emptied
for what they would put there,
and I practiced lullabies
from other mornings,
opened wide the front door,
stepped back and to the side,
but they did not come in.

Nursing Ganesha

by Alison Stone

Your purr is the one essential thing.

Pills in tuna, gravy, whipped cream, ice
cream, cream. Days a blur of bowls washed, rugs cleaned, trying
to tempt you with catnip, catgrass, velvet mice.

Death is the final gift I have for you, holding
it until the perfect time the way
my husband held a ring inside his swimming
trunks until we snorkeled through the sting-rays.

Each month he tries to hide his disappointment when
my blood begins, the way I hide my
crying while your bony body snuggles in
my lap. I gaze into your still-bright eyes,

kiss your paws and memorize the patterns of your fur.
No one can say that I am not a mother.

Our Life as a Chagall Painting
by Erin Garstka

Everywhere we are
There is color.
Birds inhabit the air.
Flowers live beyond
Vases that held them.

We never walk,
But, rising, float
To hover over a village,
Perpetual bride and groom
Holding hands and smiling.

Jugglers and acrobats
Perform for us.
At any given moment
The clouds may open.
Even angels envy us.

Poems are read,
And the gypsy woman,
Black rose behind each ear,
Touches my hair and whispers,
"But you must have a child."

Penalty

by Nancy Shiffrin

The Klementi Tribeswomen of the Albanian mountains
when they refuse the chosen groom,
risk blood-feud, stoning;
must swear never to wed;
may sit in councils of war, herd goats,
sit reclining, served by wives…
are known as Virgin.

Harry's Bar.
Meeting with Jim, editor, A MAN'S WORLD.
    "Beer here."
    "Scotch, Perrier, aspirin."
    "Bring hers right away."
The waitress winks.
Jim pinches her thigh, curves the air with his hands.
"We want the feminine viewpoint…"
    "How much?"
    "$200."
    "I know you pay more. $500."
    "$350. We don't know that a woman can write for us."

This morning I watch
a neighbor's baby lurch after a circling bird.
I think of those Albanian Virgins
served by Mamas luscious with child.
$350 will pay for my abortion.
My ovaries ache.

Petals, Ashes

by Erin Garstka

"Ladybug, Ladybug, fly away home.
Your house is on fire, your children are gone."
   —from a child's nursery rhyme

I used to imagine them playing in the attic
of our blue turn-of-the-century house,
two small shadows cast across the round window,
their blonde unruly manes streaked with light.

I even gave them names-Eve and Matthew-
and took them for walks along the river's edge,
the dog bounding happily ahead of us,
but in each scene you were absent.

At times the music of their laughter swelled
so strong I longed for laggard suns to set.
Brass weights of the clock, heavier than my heart
of stone, sank slower than burning leaves at dusk.

I greedily gave what you could not receive
in full. We were consumed, inside first,
by emptiness and could not bring forth the vine
that would bind us fast against the bleeding years.

Today I hear them calling, "Mother, Mother!"
their bright voices marring all memory.
They are my white roses pressed between pages,
petals that will never see sun nor hold the rain.

Practicing

by Alison Stone

Friends with children ask if we are trying yet,
showing photos of deliveries, bare
butts on bearskin rugs. I lie, "We're
practicing." My old eggs may not make it.

People die. The past few months it seems that
every phone call brings a funeral or
worse. Even our young cat has cancer.
My blood is a monthly disappointment.

Buddha said love attaches hooks that hold
our hearts and turn our lives to suffering.
The only cure is learning to let go,
so I try waving good-bye to our not-child,
giving back her prom night, his first snow
fall. Holding emptiness. Practicing.

River Blood

by CB Follett

I think of blood
moon-blood
that collected each month

Films in junior high,
the velvety Y of the womb
how it pillowed with blood

and waited. How the pinprick
egg set off from its ovary
and floated free

into the arms of the fallopian,
slid down the tube to the uterus,
cushioned and welcoming,

one egg per month, maybe two,
each with the potential
to look like me.

In the classroom, we watched the eggs
pause in the womb, awaiting acceptance,
but the gates opened,

lives moved on and out, the walls
sloughed their welcome into a river of red.
How many months that river,

one hundred and fifty before I was ready,
another one-fifty while I willed
the rivers to stop, begged each egg

to dam the flow, build legs and a heart:
river of hope, heartbreak river,
river without mercy.

Sestina

by Genie Hindall

From the balcony
she watched the sun
fire up over the river.
The kind of miracle
Starbucks was for coffee.
That's a business woman

speaking, a successful business woman
who earned this balcony,
who can buy coffee
futures, but not the sun
she really wants. That miracle
eludes her like a river.

Each month it's a red river.
The husband strides his woman
on the bed, the balcony,
hoping for a miracle-
for sperm to flow like coffee
not dried out by the sun.

Who was she to think the sun
would bless them in their roasted coffee
years? Tick tock. The woman
leans over the balcony
taking it all in—the miracle
of birth, the husband, a river

side home and a career. But the river
still runs red, and the sun
scorches the sperm spewed on the balcony.
And the man and woman
sip the espresso coffee
talking of all else but, the miracle.

They hold hands and still enjoy the miracle
of lovemaking by the river
and under the Caribbean sun
with exotic rums to flavor the coffee.
But does he see his woman
looking longingly from each balcony?

The cup of coffee warms the woman
but not like the miracle of a sun
to play in the river 'neath the balcony.

Setting Dobyns Straight

by Mary Sue Koeppel

(After reading "Career" by Dobyns
a former nun speaks out)

Stephen Dobyns got it all wrong—
mixed up kinds of female longing
when he saw those old nuns, veils askew,
bony shoulders burping rag dolls.

He thought, as an uninitiated might,
that nuns in 80- or 90- year senility
holding dolls must be cooing,
stroking their own phantom children.
But most nuns don't adopt senility
to find their long lost hope of cozy
motherhood. The ninety-year-old
nuns I knew rocked worn rag doll
orphans they had saved and cuddled,
preemies they had held and fed,
children they had brought to alphabets,
names of colors, naps, tastes of ice-
cream and unsweetened apple juice.

These are not the women of unfulfilled
wombs aping youngish mothers. These
liver spotted hands and blinded eyes
had rocked, and held, soothed and said,
"That's good" to Mary, John, Shuneka, Armid.
Can this man, who never birthed, understand
the overwhelming satiety of giving:
when a dottering old woman holds a baby
she does NOT mean, "I wanted motherhood."

Yet his interpretation makes a better story.

Smoke and Mirrors

by Lonnie Hull DuPont

He smokes his cigarette,
watches her in the three-way mirror.

She sits at her vanity brushing her hair
with the fine mahogany brush.

I know things about you, he says.
He runs his thumb around the ashtray,

his hooded eyes never relax.
She watches her own eyes in the mirrors,

pulls the boar's-hair of the brush
over her scalp until it hurts.

She thinks of things he does not know,
like names of children she'll never have,

or how this month
where she is from

the roses would be dead and light,
waving outside dark windows.

He says, I know you in ways
no one else can.

Yes, she says, thinking,
Simon Peter. And Zoe for a girl.

Sorrow of Barrenness

by Jachindra Kumar Rout

Behold! There
A tree is standing
On to the sky
No flower, then nothing
Meaning less, worthless of
Fragrance and beauty
Tree dreams, the water dream
In the SAHARA, the desert

Here, look, look at!
An ostracized lady
From class and clan
From moral and spirit
From occasion and austerity

Completely incomplete
Finished, Finished
Gone and disappeared

View!
Breasts are crying
Viewing swollen breasts
In the baby's lips

On the nest!
Chickens are fed
Affection, love, emotion
Oh! a pleasure, a heaven
Of a mother bird

Cry!
O'God, bless me
Pour me a baby
I'm a fallen woman
A deprived one
A dreaming one
Heart is crying
For part of lively
Flesh and blood

My sleep breaks
Listening to the cry of
A baby far away
Remotest place
Womanhood bursts into tears
Agony, sorrow, alienation
Overflow the unwomanhood I'm cheated
Betrayed by God's gift
The womb, the motherhood

I am
In a desert—mirage
In an ocean—thirsty
A cursed
A barren and infertile
The wasteland

"the soul selects its own..."

by Peggy Lin Duthie

it seems so parched to them
that, neither nun nor saint,
i would choose, *no children.*

their pity smoulders
like unnecessary summer,

their clockweight scoldings
heavy as a feast
in honor of a captive.

may i not stay priestess
to my soul's spare house?

so many ways love has, none may appear
the bitter best, and none the sweetest worst.

[The final stanza is a quotation from Countee Cullen.]

Stilled Life

by Edith Lazenby Trilling

The alone-ness pulls
me into pieces
like the fragments
of a windshield
that could not quite
stand the impact...
As if I had been
smashed behind
the wheel, my insides
fall out of my eyes
and nothingness
hangs its noose
around my neck:

    all I ever wanted
    was a baby
    to call our own.

    all I ever wanted
    was a family
    of you and me and
    that promise
    a child holds
    in every cry.

Friends feel far away.
My husband's warmth
is hidden behind
a shield of snow.

Now stands itself
up and punctures
my ears till

tears deafen
what never comes near:

Hope's prayer
spins my words
on a wheel
of time
that keeps
counting days
into years
into a lifetime
of never quite
knowing, until
seconds hold
my breath
under a veil
that won't
reveal what
I hold here.

Study in Blue

by Connie Sanderson

There is a grief beyond grieving
when the world no longer spins.
I have wandered under stars
until I could no longer breathe.

Grief settles in on winter evenings.
Snow turns blue at four o'clock.
No medicine can cure it. Sometimes art
can ease its ache. One twilight I forgot it

when the birch outside my window
donned a goldfinch necklace.
I thought for just a moment
I held the child I never had.

They All Want

by Rikki Santer

Some want me
to have a baby.
It's most logical.
I am 35.
I have a husband.
I own reservoirs of tender ways.

Most nights
a tiny, faceless mouth
sucks at me
gumming the small
of my back,
my elbows,
sometimes my breast.
This mouth woos
with moist needs
but I know its teeth—
seductive jewels now
glistening in coral sea,
to grow later
sharp and selfish
hungry for my flesh, my salt
until I become famished for its.

These nights
miles away
my father's veiled eyes watch
over my slumber,
his damp eyelashes
fanning me with his longing
for the blessing that would;
these nights
my brother's wringing hands stir
a swelling melancholy
for his young daughter
and her lost link
which I will not forge.
And these nights
my husband's stubborn back
dank from confinement
whispers hazy misgivings
with each rising breath.

In the middle of nights I rise
to sleep under my bed.
The air is dispassionate there
just right
for a gambler
with empty pockets.

They Lied to Me

by Joyce Sweeney

When I was ten I played
with rubber spiders and toy guns
They smiled at me like predators, they said

Soon you'll be interested in other things

They told me what I would be
interested in, clothes and boys—okay they were right
about the boys—but they wanted me to
get something
get something they all got and I just got

Blood

Then they said you'll regret
not having children, who will love you in your
old age, you're denying a fundamental human
drive, your husband won't stay, you'll be bitter

My answer was, slash/burn

Later they said, keep your uterus, honor your inner
Goddess, embrace your fibroids, don't let some male
Doctor castrate you, stay with our cult, be one of us, bleed
to death on our altar

Ha!

I don't have much time left, I'm not
ten anymore, I only have a few more years to be
who I really am, I am running

from the cult, I am going underground, I am
playing with rubber spiders and toy guns

You want my uterus? Take it!

Two Women Canning

by Amy Minato

By October everything kneels
or squats down. Bronze hair
crouches on your shoulders. Our hips store
extra nuts for the cold. Even the rain
carries its grey baggage and settles in.
We hunch over baskets of knobby pears
from some old tree closed in, and part
the skin's thin lip from the fruit,
ripe and sore, our fingers moist,
the pears slipping like eggs
from our knife.

It's late again you say
quartering globes into ears
which lay in quiet sterility
in their jars. *I want this child*
this time and glance away
at a squirrel on a tree
holding a sprig of moss
in its mouth, certain
to nest, to grow fur, somehow
to burrow in.

Unfettered and Alive

by Beverly Rice

No, I don't have any children, damn it.
Why do you assume that I do?
Is it because I'm black?
Is it because I'm over 30?
Hell, people assumed such about me when I was 20-something.

Is it because I have a physically demanding job?
No chick you think would do such work if she wasn't hard up
for cash to support her kids.
I tried that Suzy Officeworker crap and it paid squat.

Why must I explain, apologize for NOT contributing to the single
mom poverty train;
for NOT adding to the economic and environmental woes on the
planet?
But nooooooo—the public thinks I'm odd.

The government taxes the hell out of my single/no dependent
status but then gives credits to people with kids.
The more kids, the more tax credits.
Then the government whines about limited resources to spend
on schools, health care, housing—you know, stuff kids need.
Where's my tax break for not taking more from the government's
alleged empty wallet?

No, I don't have any children, damn it.
Children are nice but they come with a price.
I'm not financially or emotionally intact,
so I step back into the pharmacy for birth control.

Unfulfillment

by Linda S. Boerstler

How many embryos have desired
To take up residence in my womb?
How many voices have waited
To be given embodiment?
Month after month, year after year
My blood is poured out
Like a sacrifice to the one
Who is the master of my fate.
I have sought to nurture
But these breasts have never suckled
Nor have I known the filling
Of my uterus waiting
For the capture of a seed
Finally managing to take root.

Vineyards

by Ruth Moon Kempher

In spring, certain childless women
covet berries, or small words:

they find reminders in music
       or like the solitary muscadine, burgeon
       single, in soft moth-white leaves

       or the vine's growth, upwards
expectant.

          It's a cycle, the season turns
from verdant to the grapes' purple burn
ripe for harvest.
             The press waits—
in the spiral tubing there's music—

       and then, they plow pulp, seed
and skin back into earth again.

waiting for the rabbit

by Kathleen George Kearney

a rabbit came to live with me
and we had dances underneath the moon.
we ate cakes of marzipan
and drank them down with sacred rain.

i swallowed a baby
just to feel him wriggle
and jiggle and tickle inside me.

and i waited for a mother to sit down in joy
and i waited for a father to forget grammar
and i waited for a brother to admit defeat
and i waited for a friend to stand in awe
and i waited for a goddess to clap open the stars
and i waited for a god to break in heaven
and i waited for a man to walk me home.

i waited for a child
with my eyes
mine

but my mouth filled up with gossamer
and i was only throwing spiders,
lonely spiders
who cried pearls of blood
and would only eat
silver pears.

and i waited for a mother to say i was beautiful
and i waited for a father to nod gently and understand spiders
and i waited for a brother to cry in front of me
and i waited for a friend to let me die
and i waited for a goddess to bring water and sage and healing hands
and i waited for a god to close the curtains

and i waited for a lover to come laughing at the night,
        laughing into me.

i waited for a child
with my eyes
mine

but nobody came.
nobody came.
nobody came.

What Doesn't Get Told

by Mary Sue Koeppel

like the gnawing for a child, not a baby, not a tiny one,
but someone to have a conversation with at breakfast and
who will come home at night and will sometimes say,
"That's OK, Mom, because that's the way I want it, too."

Who will turn into the long-haired daughter home
for New Year's with her new child wrapped (it seems)
in red-and-white paper tissues and nibbling on a bottle
and crying sometimes to a mommy and daddy who hand her

only sometimes to a grandma, who would be you.
You'd hold her and rock her and show her the way the cat
strokes himself when he has to make himself clean for her
and the way the azalea smells like honey and the way honey

leans off a piece of warm toast and she has to lick it fast
to stop the sweetness from draining down to the carpet.
You'd show her the way her grandpa snores when he dreams of her
and the way the alligator opens its mouth to yawn, but never

to eat little ones. Together you'd watch the moon curl up to sleep,
wake to hear a crow in the morning. You'd wait for the feel
of warm water. You'd wait for the temperature of afternoon.
You'd wait and she'd watch and even the sun would be with you.

Winter Comes

by Dianna Vagianos Miller

Weeping willows whirl
into each other's arms
waltzing with wind.

I watch someone else's child,
straw-colored hair hanging.
The first colors of September.
Reds speckle the top of maple trees. Soon
color will flow like a flame spreading fire.

I long for the bare bone of tree.
Why can't my excess catch fire
and blow away becoming one with the wind?

The sun shines through green stained glass leaves.
I spread my arms around the child and wait.
And wait. Winter comes.

Watch me, I will dance in nakedness with the willow.

A Woman, Childless By Choice

by Kate Bernadette Benedict

The tree of life and the tree of life
Unloosing their moons, month after month, to no purpose.
  —Sylvia Plath

What moment is this?
I have passed into a calm finality.
I was a woman who might have children,
and now a woman who never will.

A metamorphosis-

one pictures a turbulence-
but all I feel is the empty womb, emptying.
Can anyone be less encumbered?
The lightness of my load astounds me.

And still
"the tree of life and the tree of life"
fulfill their purpose.
Readiness
comes and comes,
readiness
keeps and fills-
there is no emptiness.
I walk in plenitude, as women do.

The Women Who Have No Daughters

by Susan Landon

The women who have no daughters
are standing in the streets—
their socks unrolled,
fists held high. Ask them please
why they have no daughters.

Let them tell their tales,
but don't believe them.
Enter the cave yourself.
Pass into the darkest night of all.

Cringe before the body of a giant
intent on molesting you. Let him
tell you he loves you, pat your
head, caress your unwilling thighs.

Dare to resist: know the shame
of loving a rapist, the infamy
of hating a father, uncle, grandfather,
mother, brother, aunt.

Ask the women with no daughters
why they do not trust themselves
to nurture their daughters.
Ask them where trust has fled.

Step out on the street.
Join the women with no daughters.
Let them tell you their tales,
but don't believe them.
Enter the cave yourself.

CONTRIBUTORS

SHUSHAN AVAGYAN was born in Yerevan, Armenia. She is currently working on her master's degree in English Literature and Women's Studies, and is a recipient of the Dalkey Archive Press fellowship at the Illinois State University.

LISA BEATMAN teaches immigrant factory workers in Boston. Her work has been published in *Lonely Planet, Lilith, Hawaii Pacific Review, Powhatan Review, Rhino,* and *Manzanita.* Lisa's chapbook, *Ladies Night at the Blue Hill Spa,* was published by Bear House Publishing. She lives in (well, next to) a Roslindale cemetery, where she finds inspiration, perspective, and ticks.

KATE BERNADETTE BENEDICT is the author of *Here from Away,* a collection of poems available from CustomWords editions. She has published widely in print and online journals and serves as a moderator at Eratosphere, the web poetry forum. Visit her at katebenedict.com.

LINDA BOERSTLER returned to her hometown of Columbus, Ohio after seven years in Modesto, California. She is employed with a credit card company. However, writing is her passion. She has been published in anthologies and in website publications. She is planning to publish her first chapbook in 2005. She shares her apartment with a very verbal and demanding Jack Russell Terrier by the name of Zack.

MARIETTA W. BRATTON has been a special education teacher for thirty years. She is passionate about teaching, running, and reading. Her travels have taken her to the South Pacific islands of Samoa, Fiji, and Tonga and to the arctic community of Barrow, Alaska. She lives in Buffalo, New York with her husband, Stan.

LU CARTER is a registered nurse living in rural Nebraska. Her work has been published by several presses including the *National League for Nurses*, *The American Journal of Nursing*, *Backwaters Press*, *Outrider Press*, *Papier Mache Press*, the *Mid-America Poetry Review*, and *Potomac Review*.

ANN CEFOLA'S poetry (anncefola.com) has been published in *California Quarterly*, *Confrontation* and *The Louisville Review*; her essays in *Ape Culture* and translations in *Rhino*. In 2001, she won the Robert Penn Warren Award judged by John Ashbery. Ann also holds an M.F.A. from Sarah Lawrence College and works as a creative strategist with her own company, Jumpstart (junpstartnow.net). She and her husband, Michael, live in the New York suburbs.

M. TRACEY CHESLER is 45 years old and has lived in Syracuse, Buffalo, New York City, Chicago, Los Angeles, San Francisco, and Kapaa, Hawaii. Currently Chesler resides in Hilo, Hawaii. She earned a bachelors degree in English from the University of Hawaii at Hilo, in May 2003. On a Paul S. Honda Scholarship for International Travel, summer 2003 was spent in Ireland studying Irish literature at University College Dublin, and attending the Galway International Arts Festival. Future plans include graduate school and publication of her poetry.

KATHERINE COTTLE received her M.F.A. in creative writing from the University of Maryland at College Park. Her work has appeared in *The Greensboro Review*, *The English Journal*, *Puerto del Sol*, and *Willow Springs*. She currently tutors creative writing through the distance education program for talented youth at Johns Hopkins University. She resides in Glen Arm, Maryland.

RACHEL DACUS has a new poetry collection: *Femme au chapeau* (David Robert Books). It follows her first collection, *Earth Lessons* and two poetry CDs, *A God You Can Dance* and *Singing in the Pandaleshwar Caves*. Her writing has recently appeared in *Bellingham Review*, *Image*, *Prairie Schooner* and *Swink*. More of her writing can be found at www.dacushome.com.

BARBARA DANIELS' chapbook, *The Woman Who Tries to Believe*, won the Quentin R. Howard Prize. She received an Individual Artist Fellowship from the New Jersey State Council on the Arts, completed an M.F.A. in poetry at Vermont College, and teaches at Camden County College in New Jersey.

AMY DENGLER lives in Gloucester, Massachusetts. She is the recipient of a Robert Penn Warren Award from New England Writers. Her work has appeared in the *Atlanta Review* and other national and regional venues. Her collection of poetry, *Between Leap and Landing*, was published in 1999 by Folly Cove Books.

LONNIE HULL DU PONT lives in rural Michigan where she works as a book editor and writer. She is the author of *The Haiku Box* (Tuttle Publishing) and five poetry chapbooks from small San Francisco presses. Recently, her poems appeared in the anthologies *Boomer Girls* (University of Iowa) and *Kindled Terraces: American Poets in Greece* (Truman State University).

PEGGY LIN DUTHIE works as a calligrapher in Nashville, Tennessee. She graduated with honors from the University of Chicago and earned an M.A. in literature from the University of Michigan. Her poetry has appeared in *Astropoetica*, *KidVisions*, and other publications.

CB FOLLETT is the editor/publisher of Arctos Press, including the anthology, *GRRRRR, A Collection of Poems About Bears* and the co-editor and publisher of *RUNES, A Review of Poetry*, Winter 2001, 2002, and 2003. She is the winner of the 2001 National Poetry Book Award from Salmon Run Press and has received contest honors in the Billee Murray Denny, New Letters Prize, the Ann Stanford Prize, the Glimmer Train Poetry Contest, and several contests from the Poetry Society of America. Five poems have been nominated for a Pushcart Poetry Prize. She is an artist with artwork in many private collections nationally and internationally. She lives in Sausalito, California.

DONNA FRISK'S chapbook, *Walnut Heart*, was published by Finishing Line Press in 2004. She received her M.F.A. in Creative Writing from Antioch University-Los Angeles. Donna lives in Des Moines, Washington and enjoys hiking, cross-country skiing, gardening, photography, and reading.

ERIN GARSTKA works as an occupational therapist in home health. She and her husband, Mark, lead a poetry group in their community of Monroeville, Pennsylvania. Erin's chapbook, *The Thought of a Hat*, was published by Invisible River Publishing in 2003. Her poems have appeared in *California Quarterly*, *The Birmingham Review*, *The Lyric*, and *The Comstock Review*.

SHARON LYNN GRIFFITHS has been published in *Phoebe* (SUNY/Oneonta), *Rohwedder*, *Long Shot*, *The Paterson Literary Review*, *Exit 13*, *The Café Review*, and *California Quarterly*. Recently her work was included in *Lips* (#24/25) and *Poetry Motel*. In addition, she has been a featured reader at venues in New York and New Jersey. Sharon was born and raised in New York City, but has lived in urban New Jersey since 1990. She has been a late-night talk show host on non-commercial radio, a brown belt in karate, and a classical musician who auditioned for the Milwaukee Symphony. Sharon currently lives in Jersey City with Al Sullivan, author and staff writer for the Hudson Reporter chain of newspapers.

BARBARA HANTMAN is a resident of Whitestone, Queens. She enjoys her role as a substitute teacher in New York City public high schools, and as Corresponding Secretary for a local group of bards, the Fresh Meadows Poets. She earned her M.A. in English from Teachers College, Columbia. Barbara has published four volumes with Edwin Mellen Poetry Press: *Wistfulness and Other Foibles* (1996), *Aspects of Grace* (1998), *Shadows of Eden* (2001) and *Capullos Del Alma: Soul Buds* (2004). The last three books contain original bilingual (Spanish to English) creations. Her credits in *Midstream* include "Yom Ha-Kippurim: A Sonnet" (September/October 1999), "I Bless You" (September/October 2003) and "Hallowed Hanukkiyyah" (November/December 2003).

GENIE HINDALL'S poetry began as a result of a Poetry Workshop on Whidbey Island, Washington. Until that time letter and travel writing were her favorite forms of writing. "Write On!" by the Southern Delaware Academy of Lifelong Learning 2004 included two of her poems. She lives in Florida on a small airstrip and in Delaware with her husband, Geo and cat Spinner. Genie loves being an aunt.

DR. RHODA JANZEN has published in many literary journals, including *The Yale Review*, *The Gettysburg Review*, *Poetry Midwest*, *Borderlands*, *The Malahat Review*, *The Ledge*, and *The Cimarron Review*. In 2001 she appeared in the PBS television series *Closer To Truth*. Currently she teaches English at Hope College in Holland, Michigan. Lilith in Spring was previously published in DMQ Review.

KATHLEEN GEORGE KEARNEY was raised in Wooster, Ohio and now lives in Minneapolis, Minnesota. She is a graduate of Macalester College and United Theological Seminary of the Twin Cities. She currently works as a minister and creator/leader of life rituals. Her work can also be found in *Our Choices, Our Lives: Unapologetic Writings on Abortion*.

RUTH MOON KEMPHER, author of twenty-four collections of verse, owns and operates Kings Estate Press in St. Augustine, Florida. Retired after many years of teaching in the Florida Community College system, she now tries to travel as much as possible. While still making time for poems, she works more and more in prose, and has lately had published literary criticism, memoir and tales.

REEVES KEYWORTH lives with her husband, Jim Weston, in Tucson, Arizona. A selection of her poetry won Honorable Mention in the 2001 Pablo Neruda Prize, was published in *Nimrod*, and nominated for a Pushcart Prize. She is a recipient of a Fellowship in Fiction from the New York Foundation for the Arts. She has been a college teacher, a publicist for public television, and a copywriter. She wrote the script for *Master Smart Woman*, a film about 19th century Maine author Sarah Orne Jewett, which won a red ribbon award at the American Film Festival. She recently resigned as managing editor of a magazine in order to write fulltime; she is at work on a novel.

MARY SUE KOEPPEL, editor of *Kalliope, a Journal of Literature and Art*, teaches fulltime at Florida Community College at Jacksonville and has received Florida's highest award for teaching excellence given to a community college professor. *In the Library of Silences, Poems of Loss* (Rhiannon Press) her first poetry book, is to be followed in 2005 by *Where We Lay and Made Angels* (Canopic Press).

SUSAN LANDON lives in Somerville, Massachusetts. Her career as a software engineer/manager has given her the freedom to travel, write, and advocate for those in need. While poetry is her passion, she has also worked as a freelance journalist for publications such as the *Boston Globe*. Her poetry is widely published.

MINDY LEWIS is a writer and visual artist based in New York City. Her essays have appeared in *Newsweek, Lilith, Poets & Writers* and *Body & Soul* magazines and in two anthologies *Escaping the Yellow Wallpaper* and *Voices from the Couch*. Her memoir, *Life Inside* (Washington Square Press) was named 2003 Book of the Year by the American Journal of Nursing.

LYN LIFSHIN'S most recent prizewinning book, *Before It's Light*, earned the Paterson poetry award. It was published in 1999 by Black Sparrow Press following their publication of *Cold Comfort* in 1997. She is the subject of an award-winning documentary film, *Lyn Lifshin: Not Made of Glass*, available from Women Make Movies. Recently published books are *Another Woman Who Looks Like Me* from Black Sparrow-David Godine and *Those Days, So Persephone* from Red Hen Press. Lyn Lifshin lives between upstate New York and Virginia. Visit her at www.lynlifshin.com.

PATRICIA MC MILLEN is now "differently-childed", due to the recent acquisition of two grown stepchildren. She writes, plays banjo and presides over a farmland-owning family business in northern Illinois. "Dark Night" was originally published in *Folio* (Spring 2002) and was nominated for a Pushcart Prize.

KARLA LINN MERRIFIELD holds a Master's of Arts in Creative Writing from SUNY College at Brockport, NY. She has had poetry published in national publications such as *Earth's Daughters, Negative Capability, Mediphors*, and *Boatman's Quarterly Review* as well as in several anthologies, including *Doorways: Families, Friends and Survivors of September 11th Reflect on Living with Loss* and the new *Sacred Stones*. In 2004, Foothills Publishing published *Midst*, a collection of her poems. Merrifield teaches writing at SUNY Brockport each fall and travels widely in North America the remainder of the year.

DIANNA VAGIANOS MILLER is currently training to be a Certified Poetry Therapist. She lives in Shelton, Connecticut with her husband and three cats.

AMY KLAUKE MINATO works for Fishtrap, a nonprofit literary organization based near the Wallowa Mountains in northeast Oregon. Amy received a 2004 Oregon Literary Fellowship for her poetry, which has been published in numerous literary journals.

JENN MONROE is a native of rural Western New York. A graduate of St. Bonaventure University and the College of Saint Rose, her current work ranges from magazine articles to poetry. She also teaches writing and literature courses at colleges near her home in New Hampshire.

ROBENS NAPOLITAN is a participant in Sandpoint, Idaho's open-mike venue, "Five Minutes of Fame." She is also a member of the Sandpoint Writers Collective, a group that meets weekly to write extemporaneously. Her work has appeared in *Many Mountains Moving, Talking River Review, Orphic Lute, cold-drill, Heliotrope, Connections, Coming of Age, Women's Work, The Hungry Poet,* and *Northern Journeys.* She lives in a concrete geodesic dome by a small lake in North Idaho with her husband Tom, and their cat, Muffin. In addition to writing, her greatest love is interacting with nature. She works seasonally as a landscape gardener, getting her hands dirty as much as possible.

MARIANNE POLOSKEY is the author of the poetry collection, *Climbing the Shadows.* Her poetry has also appeared in numerous literary journals. Twenty-five of her poems have been published in *The Christian Science Monitor.* Her poem *Living in Florida* was the July 2003 Poem of the Month on the Christian Science Monitor website. Her work is also included in the recent anthologies *Inside Grief* and *American Diaspora: Poetry of Displacement.* She has written poetry book reviews for *Rattle* and *Valparaiso Poetry Review,* and was the 2003 judge for Valparaiso University's Wordfest poetry competition. She lives with her husband in Englewood, New Jersey, where she works as an independent translator.

BEVERLY RICE is a budding freelance writer who lives in Charlotte, North Carolina. She began putting pen to paper about two years ago after taking a writing class. Beverly has written gags for several cartoonists and has had a short humor piece that she wrote in her writing course published in *Short Stuff* magazine.

LAURI ROSE is a writer/nurse living in the mountains of northern California. Her writing is informed by her relationship with the land and with the rural community that surrounds her. As she enters menopause she is working with the grief of knowing she will never have children. She is also working with the joy and freedom that gives her.

JACHINDRA KUMAR ROUT is a lecturer in the English Department of Sahaspur College in India. She has published two books, *The Wicked Eye* and *Floating Dreams*. She was presented one of the "Best Poet of the Year 2003" awards from Poets International.

CONNIE SANDERSON, a retired teacher of English and French, has received a Pushcart nomination. Her works have been published in *Global City Review, Great River Review, Loonfeather, The Spoon River Poetry Review, The Wisconsin Review* and *Yankee*. She lives, writes, and gardens in a Mississippi River valley near Lynxville, Wisconsin. "Study in Blue" was published in *Lyrical Iowa*.

RIKKI SANTER'S work has appeared in regional and national publications including, *Ms. Magazine, Poetry &, Potomac Review*, and most recently *Poetry East*. An anthology of poetry published by Ground Torpedo Press also included her work. She lives in Ohio. "They All Want" was previously published by the *Alabama Literary Review*.

JACQUELINE SENTMANAT is 38 years old and lives in Houston, Texas. She is employed as a CPA, but has dabbled with writing as a form of both therapy and self-reflection. "The Gypsy" was based upon a true event in her life. She enjoys rollerblading, reading and listening to music.

NANCY SHIFFRIN is the author of *The Holy Letters* (poems) and *My Jewish Name* (essays), greatunpublishedauthors.com, 2000 and 2002 respectively. Through Creative Writing Services, she helps aspiring writers achieve publication and personal satisfaction. Visit her at earthlink.net/-nshiffrin/.

ALISON STONE'S poems have appeared in *The Paris Review, Poetry, Ploughshares* and a variety of other journals and anthologies. She has been awarded *Poetry*'s Frederick Boch Prize and *New York Quarterly*'s Madeline Sadin Award. Her first book, *They Sing at Midnight*, won the 2003 *Many Mountains Moving* Poetry Award and was recently published. She is also a painter and the creator of The Stone Tarot.

JOYCE SWEENEY was born and raised in Dayton, Ohio. She is the author of eleven novels for young adults; including *Waiting for June*, Marshall Cavendish, 2003 and *Takedown*, Marshall Cavendish, 2004. Her books have been recognized by the American Library Association, the New York Public Library and Working Mother Magazine as best books for teenagers. Joyce is also a writing teacher and has twelve students who have published books of their own. Her hobbies include poetry, Native American studies and pro-wrestling. She lives in Coral Springs, Florida with her husband Jay and cat, Macoco.

ALISON TOWNSEND is the author of two books of poetry, *The Blue Dress* (White Pine Press) and *What the Body Knows* (Parallel Press). Her poetry and nonfiction have appeared in many anthologies and journals, including *Boomer Girls, Claiming the Spirit Within, Are You Experienced, The North American Review, Calyx, Nimrod* and *The Southern Review*. She teaches at the University of Wisconsin-Whitewater and lives in the farm country outside Madison.

EDITH LAZENBY TRILLING has been writing since a teenager. She has been published in *The Black Buzzard Review, The Metropolitan, Penumbra, The Black Creek Review* and *The Timbercreek Review*. She mainly writes poetry, but plays with other genres as well. She is a yoga teacher, leasing agent, and bead jeweler. She graduated from the University of Maryland at College Park, and has lived in both the Boston-Cambridge area as well as North Carolina. Edith has been living in the District of Columbia since 1987 where she resides with her husband.

CAROL TUFTS teaches English and Creative Writing at Oberlin College. Her poems have appeared in a number of little magazines including, *Poetry, Columbia, Poem*, and *The Comstock Review*, as well as the recent anthology, *Orpheus and Company*. "Grief's Place" appeared in *Iowa Woman*, and "Memorial Lights" in *Poetica*.

978-0-595-37124-2
0-595-37124-8

Printed in the United States
55407LVS00005B/251